Historical Atlases of South Asia,
Central Asia, and the Middle East ™

A HISTORICAL ATLAS OF

ISRAEL

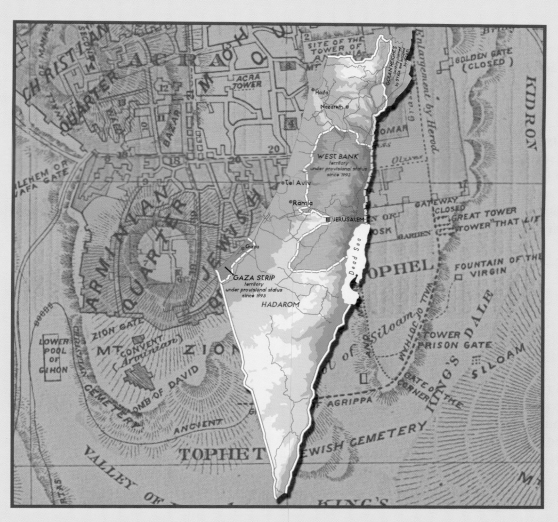

Amy Romano

The Rosen Publishing Group, Inc., New York

To facilitate understanding, acceptance, and peace.

Published in 2004 by The Rosen Publishing Group, Inc.
29 East 21st Street, New York, NY 10010

Copyright © 2004 by The Rosen Publishing Group, Inc.

First Edition

Library of Congress Cataloging-in-Publication Data

Romano, Amy.
A historical atlas of Israel/ Amy Romano
p. cm. — (Historical atlases of South Asia, Central Asia and the Middle East)
Summary: Maps and text chronicle the history of Israel from the Biblical period to the events of the present day.
Includes bibliographical references.
ISBN 0-8239-3978-2
1. Israel—History—Maps for children. 2. Israel—Maps for children. [1. Israel—History.
2. Atlases.]
I. Title. II. Series.

G2236.S1R66 2003

2003055005

Manufactured in the United States of America

Cover Image: The lands later known as Israel and its capital city Jerusalem *(current and nineteenth-century maps, center)* have been host to many civilizations, including the Canaanites, as evidenced in this jar fragment from 1600 BC *(top right)*. Israel's first prime minister, David Ben-Gurion *(left)* served from 1949 to 1953 and again from 1955 to 1963, while Ariel Sharon *(bottom)* currently holds this position.

Contents

LEBANON

GOLAN HEIGHTS
territory claimed
by Syria and occupied
by Israel

GOLAN HEIGHTS

MEDITERRANEAN
SEA

Nazareth

WEST

WEST BANK AND
GAZA STRIP
territories
under provisional status
since 1993

Tel Aviv

Al Ghawr / Jordan

Ramla

JERUSALEM

Bethlehem

BANK

Dead Sea

GAZA STRIP

Gaza

JORDAN

EGYPT

SYRIA

SAUDI
ARABIA

INTRODUCTION

A s revered as it has been ravaged, Israel's history is a complex weave of conflict and harmony. Located at the center of three continents — Asia, Europe, and Africa — modern Israel lies at the eastern edge of the Mediterranean Sea. Predominantly a Jewish state, Israel is entirely surrounded by Arab and Islamic countries.

Israel shares its eastern border with Jordan and the Palestinian territory known as the West Bank. Lebanon borders Israel to the north, and Syria lies to its northeast. Egypt is Israel's southwestern neighbor, and the Mediterranean Sea embraces its entire western border. The southernmost tip of Israel also falls on water, extending to the Gulf of Aqaba, an arm of the Red Sea.

Predestined by its location to play a more significant role in the region's history than its modest size might suggest, the

Israel was created following the British withdrawal from Palestine after World War II. A 1948 partition was decided by the United Nations but ultimately rejected by Palestinians. Tensions between the two groups continued, eventually developing into a series of wars and uprisings. Subsequently, territories gained by the Israelis, such as the Golan Heights, and portions of the West Bank and Gaza Strip have been occupied and/or settled since the 1960s. The 1980s and 1990s brought about a series of peace treaties between Israel and other nations, including Egypt, Jordan, and Syria. Violence continues to periodically erupt, however, between Israelis and Palestinians.

This human skull dates back to the earliest Neolithic settlements in Palestine, or approximately 7000 BC. The Neolithic Period (8000–4500 BC) is the period in the Stone Age that archaeologists and anthropologists believe was the time in which settlers domesticated plants and animals and began making tools and pottery. This skull was found in Jericho during the 1980s and is now housed in the Jordan Archaeological Museum in Amman, Jordan. Jericho is considered the world's oldest community, having developed about 1,000 years before Mesopotamia (Iraq).

territory now known as Israel has endured centuries of invasion and conquest. At one time or another, all or part of Israel has been a Roman province, a crusader kingdom, a territory of both Egypt and Turkey, and a British protectorate. Alexander the Great, Constantine, and Napoléon Bonaparte, as well as the spiritual figures Abraham, Muhammad, Moses, and Jesus have all left an indelible mark on the country's evolution.

The recorded history of Israel begins in the Bible, around 2000 BC, with the story of Abraham. Archaeologists, however, have evidence of human civilizations in this region dating back 1.2 million years at Ubeidiya in the Jordan Valley. Located in the long-disputed area of the West Bank, Jericho is the most famous of these prehistoric cities, dating between 6000 and 10000 BC.

The burden of a young country having such an ancient history is not a comparison that goes unnoticed by Israel's population of six million. Known as the State of Israel since 1948, present-day struggles between Israel and surrounding Arab nations have haunted the region for centuries. Israel is a country where everyday interactions are often shaped by ancient conflicts.

Referred to at various times throughout history as Canaan, Judah (Judea), and Palestine, Israel has witnessed the birth of world religions. It has benefited from and suffered through history's greatest empires. Israel lies at the center of three major religions (Judaism, Christianity, and Islam) and has been the battleground in the world's longest-running conflict. Israel is an ever evolving storybook of human history.

1 ANCIENT ISRAEL

Israel's history begins nearly 10,000 years ago with the birth of civilization. Known as Canaan, historians agree that these lands are the present-day sites of both Lebanon and Israel. This assumption is so universal, in fact, that it is nearly impossible to discuss Israel's ancient history without referencing the biblical stories of Abraham, Moses, David, and Solomon. The impact of these thousand-year-old stories of devotion and betrayal, sibling rivalry, and hierarchy is still felt today.

With Trust in One God

Around 2000 BC, Abraham, the son of a Mesopotamian merchant family in Ur (modern Iraq), led a group of citizens known as Hebrews from Mesopotamia. The Hebrews were trying to escape fighting between Egyptian forces and the ruling Sumerians. The Canaanites, a Semitic people who inhabited Canaan, called Abraham and his people *habiru*, which translated to "wanderers." "Hebrew" is derived from this word.

As recorded in the Bible, God told Abraham to lead the Hebrews out of Mesopotamia to neighboring Canaan. Before doing so, God and Abraham made a covenant (agreement). The terms of the covenant set the stage for centuries of fighting surrounding Jewish

This fragment of a painted jar dates to 1600 BC during the Canaanite Period (3000–1200 BC), otherwise known as the Middle Bronze Age. The Canaanites were a Semitic people who traded with neighboring settlements in Mesopotamia and Egypt, domesticated animals, crafted terra-cotta wares such as this one, and established various colonies, such as one that existed on the island of Cyprus.

claims on Israel as their divine homeland. It also dramatically affected the evolution of religions in general. As the idea of polytheism (the worship of multiple gods) was abandoned and monotheism (the belief in a single god) was embraced, these conflicts deepened.

God promised to protect Abraham and his people in their new homeland of Canaan. They journeyed to the promised land and settled there, continuing to herd animals. The Hebrews remained relatively undisturbed for three hundred years until drought and famine forced them to migrate. Poor living conditions caused Abraham's grandson, Joseph, to lead the Hebrews—largely referred to as Israelites—into Egypt. Although

welcomed at first, the Egyptian pharaohs (kings) ultimately enslaved the Israelites for nearly four hundred years. It was on the backs of the enslaved Israelites that the Egyptian pyramids were built.

In 1300 BC, the longing of the Israelites for the promised land became stronger. Moses, one of Judaism's prophets, acting on what he believed to be direct instructions from God, rallied the Israelites. Moses persuaded the pharaoh to let the Israelites return to Canaan. This Exodus would take forty years. During this time, biblical recordings recount the delivery of the Torah and the Ten Commandments to Moses atop Mount Sinai. A second covenant with God further solidified the belief that the lands known today as Israel belonged to the Jews.

Rise of the Israelites

As the Israelites were returning to claim Canaan as their promised land, a group of warlike seafaring wanderers known as Philistines were settling south of Canaan along the Mediterranean coast. Philistine power would ultimately give rise to the name of Palestine.

Upon the Israelites' return to Canaan, they met intense resistance from the native Canaanites. A long series of battles followed. By the early eleventh century BC, the twelve

Judaism

Neither theologians nor historians can pinpoint a date for the founding of Judaism. It is widely accepted, however, that it originated in Israel. It is the religious culture of the Jews, and one of the world's oldest monotheistic religions.

Followers of Judaism believe that nothing humanity experiences is whimsical; everything ultimately has meaning because a single divine intelligence stands behind it. A second major concept in Judaism is that of the covenant, or contractual agreement, between God and the Jewish people. It is the belief that in return for devotion to God and the agreement to obey his laws, He would protect them.

Much Jewish thought has been preoccupied with the problem of affirming justice in the face of injustice. In time, this problem was worsened by the belief that virtue would be rewarded and sin punished by divine judgment. This justice would be handed down when God sent his Messiah to redeem the Jews. Known as messianism, this idea has always been significant in Judaism.

This mosaic of a menorah dates from the fourth century AD. Today, Jews light the menorah when celebrating Hanukkah, an eight-day festival that occurs in November-December of every year. The holiday, sometimes called the Festival of Lights, commemorates the rededication of the Holy Temple in Jerusalem in 165 BC. In Hebrew, the word "hanukkah" means "dedication."

Israelite tribes had defeated Canaanite forces and claimed much of the territory. Success against the Philistines was not as easily won.

The strength of the Philistine army led the Israelites to unify and choose a king. As their first leader, they chose Saul, who reigned from 1023 to 1004 BC. Although Saul won many military victories, it was his son-in-law, David—the fabled slayer of Goliath—who succeeded in unifying the twelve Israelite tribes to form the first nation of Israel.

From Father to Son to Son

After his father-in-law's death in 1004 BC, David became king of Israel and reigned until 965 BC. During this time he captured

This nineteenth-century engraving of King Solomon, by Gustave Doré, was taken from a 1865 illustrated Bible commissioned by British publishers. As the king of Israel from around 965 to 928 BC, he greatly expanded his empire, dividing it into twelve sections. His use of slave labor during the construction of Solomon's Temple led to growing resentment of his policies.

Jerusalem from the Canaanites and proclaimed the holy city as his capital. David is also credited with creating the Ark of the Covenant—the chest believed to contain the stone tablets on which the Ten Commandments were inscribed—and conquering the Philistines. Under David's rule, the Israelites developed a national identity and became a powerful political state.

David's second son, Solomon, became king of Israel around 965 BC and reigned for forty-four years. Solomon continued his father's successes, ultimately extending his domain north to the Euphrates River and south to the Red Sea. He also reorganized his father's kingdom and governed largely through administrative, not military, means. Solomon divided Israel into twelve parts. He made slaves of the remaining Canaanites and formed alliances with Egypt and Hiram, king of Tyre (present-day Lebanon).

Within Jerusalem, Solomon also built the first temple for the worship of God. It took seventy thousand men seven years to complete. Solomon's Temple and the city's royal palaces became the center of Solomon's empire.

A House Divided

Solomon's designs came at a high price. His harsh treatment of the Israelites and the heavy taxes he imposed in order to maintain the city bred discontent among them. When he died in 922 BC, an open rebellion erupted across Israel and the kingdom divided in two.

In the north, Israel was ruled by foreign kings from Samaria, an ancient city in Palestine located north of Jerusalem, before being conquered by the Assyrians in 721 BC. The Assyrians were great warriors from the upper Tigris River in Mesopotamia, now a region in

This map shows King Solomon's divided kingdom after his death in 922 BC. The kingdom was originally divided into two sections: Israel to the north and Judah to the south. To the far north, the Aramaeans controlled the land from present-day Syria to the banks of the Euphrates River, while the Phoenicians were confined to the Mediterranean coast.

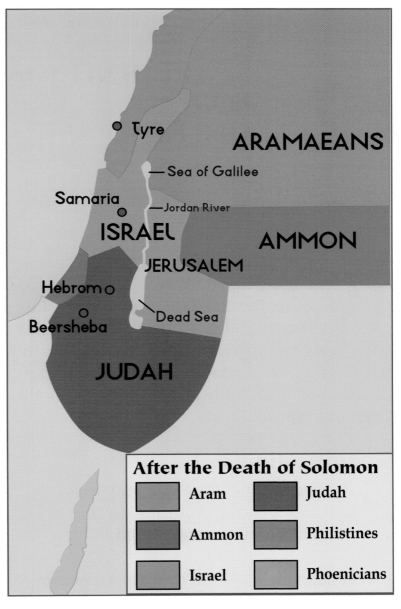

After the Death of Solomon

Aram		Judah	
Ammon		Philistines	
Israel		Phoenicians	

northern Iraq. After the Assyrians invaded, the ten tribes of Israelites that comprised the kingdom of Israel were exiled. They scattered and would never again become part of a unified Jewish kingdom.

Southern Israel became known as Judah (Judea), with Jerusalem remaining as its capital. Judah submitted without violence to Assyrian advances and was allowed to remain independent. As a result, Judah continued to thrive. Unfortunately, in 586 BC, King Nebuchadnezzar of Babylonia, also in Mesopotamia, captured Judah and burned Jerusalem, razing Solomon's Temple. After the destruction, Nebuchadnezzar exiled the Israelites of Judah back to Babylonia, where they were enslaved for some forty years.

2 SEARCHING FOR UNITY

When the Babylonian Empire fell in 537 BC to the Persians, the Persian king Cyrus I, allowed the exiles to return to Judah. Once a powerful commercial entity, the Jews—as the people of Judah were now called—inhabited only a small province of the Persian Empire.

Reunification and Rebirth

The Jews rebuilt Jerusalem and Solomon's Temple under Cyrus, but they did not regain independence. They were unified only in their religious beliefs.

Persian rule in Judah came to an end in 331 BC with the advance of a Macedonian general named Alexander the Great. At the time, Alexander reigned over Judah and Palestine, and the Macedonian kingdom stretched from Greece to India. After Alexander's death in

This panoramic map of Palestine was painted in 1853 on a Shivite, a decorative plaque on the eastern wall of a synagogue to indicate the direction of prayer toward Jerusalem. Originally found in Constantinople (present-day Istanbul), Turkey, it is now part of the collection of the Metropolitan Museum of Art in New York.

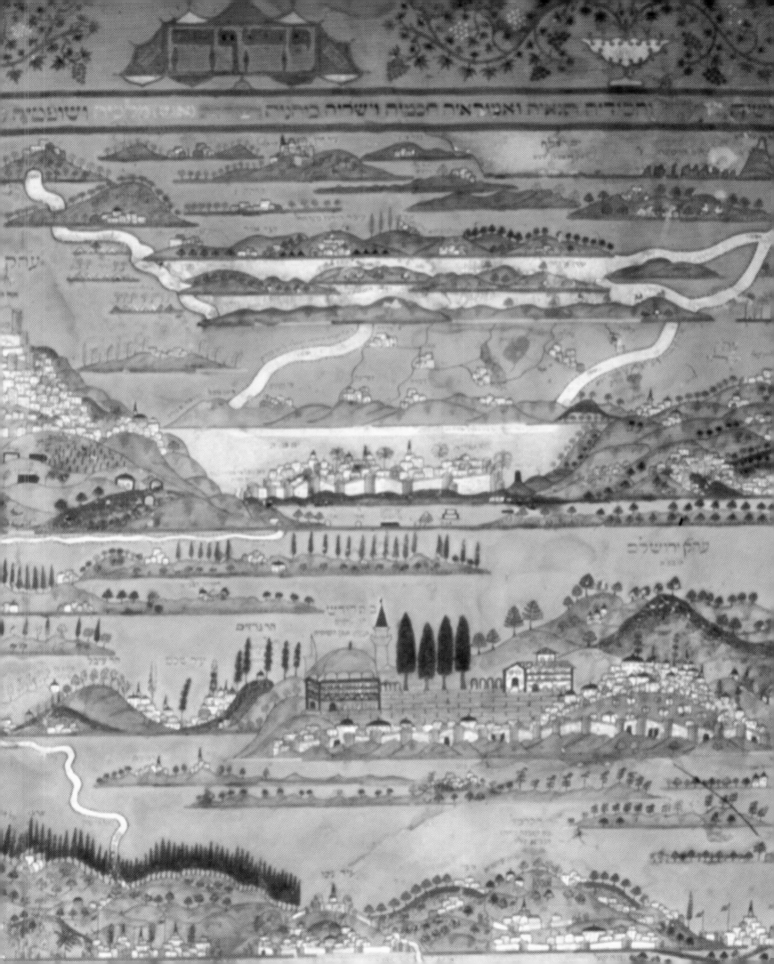

BLACK SEA

CASPIAN SEA

MACEDONIA

MEDITERRANEAN SEA

Tigris

Nineveh

Euphrates

Damascus

Babylon

Susa

Alexandria

Memphis

EGYPT

PERSIAN

ARABIA

RED SEA

Medina

Nile

Mecca

Route of Alexander the Great (334–323 BC)

	Macedonian Empire
——	**Alexander's route (334-323 BC)**

This map shows the extent of the Macedonian Empire under Alexander the Great. The inset map shows how Alexander's territories were divided into kingdoms after his death in 323 BC. His immediate followers, known as the Diadochi, included Antigonus I, Ptolemy I, Seleucus I, and Lysimachus. (The conflicts between them for territory formerly under Alexander are known as the War of the Diadochi.) Divisions of his empire under Cassander and Chandragupta came later.

Alexandria Eskhata
(Kokard)

Bactra

Alexandria Aeria
(Herat)

Taxila

Alexandria
(Kandahar)

Pasargadae

Persepolis

Pura

Black
Sea

Byzantium

The Division of Alexander's Empire Between 306–303 BC

1	Antigonus I	4	Ptolemy I
2	Seleucus I	5	Cassander
3	Lysimachus	6	Chandragupta

5

3

1

Rhodes

Caspian
Sea

Alexandria Aeria
(Herat)

2

Crete

Cyprus

Mediterranean
Sea

Susa

Babylon

Persepolis

Gaza

Alexandria

Memphis

EGYPT

ARABIA

Tigris

Euphrates

Persian Gulf

Pura

6

Pattala

Nile

Red Sea

Medina

Arabian Sea

4

Mecca

323 BC, his kingdom divided. The Seleucids won control over the land that extended from present-day Israel and Lebanon to Mesopotamia and Persia. Judah fell to the Ptolemies and remained under their control until 198 BC when the armies of Antiochus IV of Syria invaded.

During his reign in Judah, Antiochus tried to suppress Judaism. Under the leadership of Jewish priest Mattathias and his sons the Maccabees, the Jews revolted and drove Antiochus from Jerusalem. In 164 BC, Judas Maccabee led a revolt of the Jewish lower classes against the Syrian army and regained Judah's independence. This event is commemorated today by the observance of Hanukkah.

Judah was again an independent kingdom. The Maccabees sanctified Solomon's Temple and a century of Jewish prosperity followed. Unfortunately, this would be the last such period for nearly 2,000 years.

Romans, Religion, and Revolts

In 63 BC, two brothers on opposite sides of a brewing Jewish civil war had so divided Judah that when Roman armies invaded, the kingdom was unable to defend itself. With the advance of the great Roman general Pompey, 300 years of Roman rule in the region began. During this period Judah and the surrounding territory was called Palestine.

Under Roman administration, Palestine remained a self-governed province with its own kings. The best known of these kings was Herod the Great, who reigned from 37 to 4 BC. During this period Palestine flourished. The Second Temple of Jerusalem was built, and grand cities were constructed.

Herod's sons, however, were not skillful rulers. In AD 6, to bring an end to the chaos caused by the weakening administration, the Romans installed a puppet government (one where appointed leaders are mere figureheads and have no power). The most famous of these officials was Pontius Pilate, whose name is infamously tied to the trial and crucifixion of Jesus Christ. Jesus was born in Bethlehem during the early years of Roman rule.

As time passed, the Jews became increasingly unhappy with their Roman governors. By AD 66, a group

The Romans incorporated Judah (present-day Israel) into their empire in 63 BC and placed the Jewish kingdoms under the control of separate kings, of whom Herod the Great is the most famous. He was the leader of the Jews from 37 to 4 BC. The ruins seen here are from one of his few palaces in Jerusalem.

of Jewish nationalists known as Zealots staged the first of two Jewish rebellions. After three years of terrorist attacks against the Roman legion, Titus, the local Roman commander, succeeded in defeating the Zealots. His armies destroyed Jerusalem and demolished the Second Temple. Titus left only one wall of the temple standing. Today this wall is known

The mountaintop known as Masada rises out of the Judean desert and is revered as a place of Jewish independence. After the fall of Jerusalem, nearly 1,000 Zionist resisters fled Jerusalem to Masada, where they withstood a two-year Roman-led siege. Finally, seeing no alternative by AD 73, 960 individuals chose to commit suicide rather than be forced into a life of slavery. Seven people survived to tell the story of those who had chosen to end their lives. Today, many Jews make a pilgrimage to Masada to honor their heritage.

as the Wailing Wall because it is where vigils are held to mourn the temple's destruction.

With this defeat the Zealots retreated to Masada, a mountaintop fortress built by Herod outside of Jerusalem near the Dead Sea. Masada fell in AD 73, ending the existence of a recognized Jewish kingdom. Although Jewish forces would revolt again between AD 132 and 135, an independent Jewish state would not reemerge for more than 1,000 years.

An Identity Lost

To protect against future Jewish uprisings, Roman forces systematically put Jewish leaders to death and disturbed Jewish communities throughout Palestine. The Jews of Palestine were dispersed far and wide. This scattering came to be known as the Diaspora, derived from the Greek word for dispersion. Jews called it the Golah. To make matters worse, Jerusalem was

Christianity

Christianity is the religion based on the life and teachings of Jesus Christ (4 BC–AD 37). It is currently the second-largest religion in the Middle East with about fourteen million adherents.

The religion originated approximately 2,000 years ago in Judah (present-day Israel). Christians are members of one of three major sects (groups)—Roman Catholic, Protestant, or Eastern Orthodox. These sects have different beliefs about Jesus and his teachings. Most Christians believe God sent Jesus into the world as the savior, and that humanity can achieve salvation through Jesus. The influence of Christianity can be seen throughout history in art, literature, and philosophy.

This mosaic of Jesus Christ dates from the fourteenth century. Mosaics were often applied to interior domes of Christian churches, and depictions of Christ were often prominent. Often highly luminous and embellished with golden tiles, the mosaics from this era are recalled for their brilliance, artistic craftsmanship, and beauty.

renamed Aelia Capitolina by the Romans, and all remnants of Jewish culture were destroyed.

Jews who were not executed at the hands of the Romans were either exiled or enslaved. Others fled to Europe and parts of North Africa. Some Jewish communities continued to exist within Palestine, mostly in Galilee. Galilee comprised all of what was then northern Palestine west of the Jordan River and the Sea of Galilee (Lake Tiberias).

Despite the oppression the Jews suffered at the hands of the Romans and later as a result of the spread of Christianity and Islam, Jewish culture remained. Christianity soon took hold in the region, however, and Jewish presence in the Holy Land waned.

Byzantine Rule

In AD 330, Palestine came under the control of the Byzantine Empire. Little would change for Palestine administratively, but Constantine's

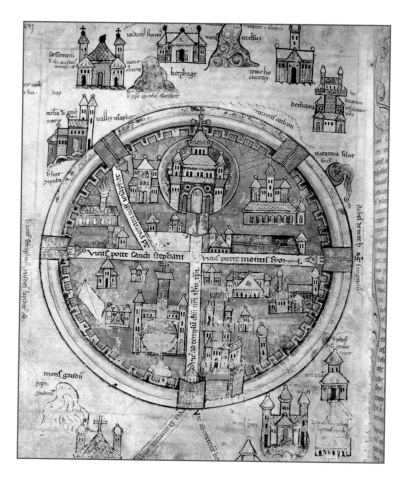

This medieval map of Jerusalem, circa 1099, was taken from Robert Monk's *Chronicle of the Crusades*, written about twenty-five years after the First Crusade (1095–1099). In it, Monk describes the speech given by Pope Urban II at the Council of Clarmont in 1095 that inspired the Crusades. One of the first Christian maps of Jerusalem, it is pictorial in style, portraying the Holy Land as a circular walled city in a pattern typical of maps of this period.

adoption of Christianity as the official religion of his empire would have dramatic results.

While under Byzantine rule, Constantine, largely through the pilgrimages of his mother, Empress Helena, promoted the total Christianization of the Roman Empire. Many churches were built, and many of the sites where Christ had lived or was believed to have performed miracles were turned into shrines.

But for a fourteen-year interruption beginning in 614 when Persian armies swept into Palestine and captured Jerusalem, Byzantine rule dominated until the seventh century. In 641, Jerusalem would fall to a new group of invaders who called themselves Arabs. The Arabs traced their ancestry to the nomadic tribes of the Arabian Peninsula. Arabs would control Palestine for some 400 years.

3 THE LAST EMPIRES

In 641, an Arab bedouin (nomadic) army, led by Caliph Omar, the second caliph of the Islamic Empire, captured Jerusalem from the Byzantines. Over the next 400 years, they turned Palestine into an Islamic center. It is considered ironic by some people that in the Holy Land, where Christ was born, preached, and died, Christians are now a minority.

The Rise of Islam

Muslims built Islamic mosques throughout Palestine, concentrating in Jerusalem. Like Christians and Jews, Muslims also revered Jerusalem as a holy city.

Although Muslims allowed the practice of Christianity and Judaism, these people did not have the same rights as Arabs had. Over time, the population accepted the Islamic culture of their rulers, and the Arab, Jewish, and Christian communities have since sought control over the Holy Land. In 661, a Muslim civil war created a split in the Muslim world that lasts to this day. As a result of this conflict, two sects of Islam, Sunni and Shia, were born.

With the election of Caliph Ali in 661, the Sunni Muslim Umayyad dynasty was established. Eighty years later, the Islamic world stretched from Narbonne, a city in southern France, to Samarkand in present-day Uzbekistan. By 750, another Sunni

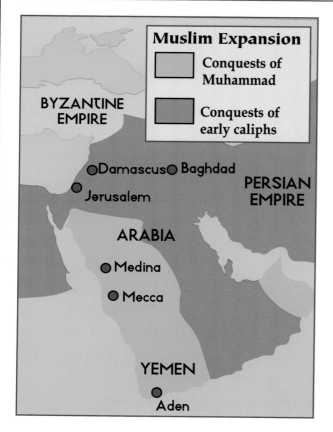

Muslim Expansion

- Conquests of Muhammad
- Conquests of early caliphs

BYZANTINE EMPIRE

Damascus Baghdad

Jerusalem

PERSIAN EMPIRE

ARABIA

Medina

Mecca

YEMEN

Aden

The power and endurance of Islam was so great that it gained converts over three continents (Asia, Africa, and Europe) within a few centuries of Muhammad's death in AD 632. Palestine, and therefore Jerusalem, was largely absorbed into the Arab Empire under Omar between 634 and 664. Under both the Umayyad and 'Abbasid dynasties, Arabs would support and spread their faith while incorporating some of the culture from territories that they conquered. Arabs absorbed the heritage of the ancient Egyptians, Persians, and Greeks, and translated centuries of important literary, scientific, and mathematical works into Arabic.

destroyed Jerusalem's Church of the Holy Sepulchre.

The Crusades

The expansion of Islam was not limited to Palestine. Muslim forces were

dynasty, the 'Abbasids, had come to power by overthrowing the ruling Umayyads. Now ruling from Baghdad, the 'Abbasid dynasty was an immense bureaucracy.

The 'Abbasids would rule, although not unchallenged, until 977. At this time, the Shia Fatimids from Egypt advanced northward under a leader known as al-Hakim and captured most of Palestine, including Jerusalem. Under the Fatimid caliph, trade and the economy flourished. The religious tolerance that the region had enjoyed for more than 300 years, however, was no more. As a demonstration of al-Hakim's dislike of Christianity, he

Islam

Islam is the name given to the religion preached by the prophet Muhammad, beginning in AD 600. It is the world's second-largest religion after Christianity. In Islam, there are three historic divisions built on the central concept of *tawhid*, or the oneness of God. Any person who follows the teachings of Islam is called a Muslim.

The majority of Muslims belong to the Sunni sect. Sunni Muslims believe that Muhammad's successor, or caliph, should become the Muslim ruler after his death. Most conservative or fundamentalist Muslims are Sunnis who follow a strict approach to religion, rejecting modern and popular interpretation of Islamic law. The next largest division is the Shia, whose members are called Shiites. Shiites believe that only blood descendants of Muhammad should be permitted to rule.

The map on this page illustrates the routes of crusaders during the eleventh and twelfth centuries. The First Crusade (1095–1099) led the Christians through present-day Syria and Turkey to conquer several Muslim cities, including Jerusalem in 1099. During the Second Crusade (1147–1149), Christians attempted to take Damascus but failed. By this time, Muslims under Saladin had united, and they retook Jerusalem in 1187. During the Third Crusade (1189–1192), Christian forces occupied Cyprus and the city of Acre in present-day Lebanon.

so strong that by 656, all of Persia and the Middle East were ruled from the Muslim capital in Medina, Arabia. Muslim conquest was, in fact, sweeping the Holy Land.

In 1095, Pope Urban II launched an appeal for a unified European force to intervene and bring a stop to the spread of Islam. The goal was to restore Christian rule in Palestine and to liberate Jerusalem. This Christian holy war was known as the Crusades.

Two years later, some 100,000 European troops arrived in Constantinople. In 1099, they seized Jerusalem, slaughtering every man, woman, and child. Within forty years, there was a strip of crusader-controlled land that ran from southern Turkey to Aqaba.

In 1144, Muslim forces in northern Syria started to diminish crusader territories. Arab success inspired a wave of resistance that

Quarta etas mũdi

victoriam non humane virtutis sed diuine gratie fateretur. In ea vastatione fuit ea hominũ strages ea fa/
mes miseroz funesta necessitas: Que si ex ordine noscere cupis Iosephum lege. Non audita sed visa et cõ/
munia sibi cũ ceteris referentẽ. Aeniẽs deuicҍ Tit⁹ romã cũ patre suo Uespasiano triũphũ celeberrimuz
egit. Simonẽ qui vrbis excidij causa fuit in triũpho pductũ postea laqueo p totã ciuitate traxerunt multis
confossuz vulnerib⁹ interfecerut. Uespasian⁹ templũ pacis edificauit vbi iudeoz preciosioza instrumẽta vi
delicet tabulas legis penetraliũ vela.z alia multa reposuit. Ea aũt vrbs vsҍ ad adriani principis tpa la/
tronũ sicarioҏũcҍ facta est receptaculũ. Et p quiquagĩta annos: deinde ciuitatis mãsere reliquie. Quã po
stea Adrianus impatoz menib⁹z edificijs instaurãs de suo noie helyam appellauit: et diu⁹ Hieronim⁹ ad
paulinũ scrib̃ t ab̃adriani tpibus vsҍ ad impium Constãtini p annos circiter. clxxx. In loco resurrectiõis
simulacrũ iouis in crucis rupe statua ex marmoze veneris a gentilib⁹ posita colebat. Estimãtib⁹ psecutõis
auctozib⁹ cҍ tollerẽt nobis fidẽ resurrectiõis z crucis: si loca sancta p ydola polluissent. Maiozes dein no/
stri gloziosissimã ciuitatẽ diu possessaz. tandẽ amiserũt. Karolus eṁ magn⁹ multo sudoze primo vrbẽ illaz
vendicauit deinde pditam recupauit Gothefridus. Ad quã retinendã etiaz Conradus cesar: Ludouicusҍ
rex francoҏ nõ dubitarũt coactis exercitib⁹ in asiam pficisci. At cũ nr̃i principes postea desidie sese dederũt
neҍ hierosolima nec Antioẽbia in potestate nr̃a remãsere. Heu pudoz: heu doloz fons z ozigo nr̃e salutis
defecit. Templũ illud Salomonis fama clarũ: in quo domin⁹ tociẽs pdicauit: Bethleẽ in qua nat⁹est. Cal
uariam in qua crucifix⁹ Ipsius crucis possidẽt inimici. Sepulcruz dñi gloriosum in quo ppter nos obdoz
miuit in dño: saraceni in ptate habẽt. Et nisi velint xpiani inuisere nõ possunt. En ipam dei viuẽtis ciuita/
tem officinasҍ nr̃e redẽptiõis: quã de⁹ nr̃ miraclĩs illustrauit z pprio sanguie dedicauit: In q̃ pme resurre/
ctionis flozes apparuerũt: Machometi satellites oculcãt. Et ea vrbs nũc scelerate gentĩ impio paret.

DESTRVCCIO? IHEROSOLIME

li etas IIic incipit et oztum babuit a captiuitate iudeozum in Babiloniam duratqzvlqz
su domini nostri natiuitatem per annos. 590. quis in bac supputatione aliqui aliter
inde qui recte captiuitatis annos numerare voluerint ab vndecimo Sedechie regni an
it.tunc septuaginta captiuitatis annos in secūdū Barij annuz terminabunt. Josephus
us a.13. Josie regis vsqz ad tercium Cyri regis annuz. Nonnulli ab vltimo regis Joa/
ant vsqz ad vltimum Cyri annum. At sane sentiendo septuaginta illi anni qui in tercio
no terminantur. propzie captiuitatis iudaice anni dicuntur. Illi vero qui in scdō Barij
e complete transmigratiōis sunt. Et bec principaliozr et precipua sacre scripture era ba/
no ab exozdio mōi. 4610.A diluuio aūt. 2369.A natiuitate abrabe.1427.Ac vigesi/
arquini romanozum regis. Regnantibus etiam apud IIedos astyage. apud IIacedo
qz lydos alyacte:et apud egiptios vaphre:et apō Caldeos nabuchodonosoz pmus.

gitur bebzeozum que fuit exterminium populi bierusalē bic incipit. Et per annos. 70.
um enim populus israel iam multis tempozibus ydolis seruiendo : etiam effusionem
nnocentium se grauiter impiasset : volens deus generationem buius populi deperire :
um captiuitatem eundem populum in regno caldeozum statuit sustinere. IIac ratione vt
numero nouus populus a memozatis peccatis imminis ad renouationem bierusalez

This print, one of the 1,800 woodcuts from the *Nuremberg Chronicle*, depicts an imaginary view of Jerusalem looking westward from the Mount of Olives, a mountainside cemetery. The *Nuremberg Chronicle*, compiled by Hartmann Schedel, is a history of the world from its creation until 1493 (the year of the book's publication) and remains one of the world's most famous fifteenth-century books, along with the Gutenberg Bible. It was printed in Germany with the assistance of the artist Albrecht Dürer, who used xylography, or the art of making engravings on wood for the purposes of printing. This view of Jerusalem shows the city in six various stages of destruction. Solomon's Temple is seen here in flames.

united the Muslim world. The Muslim goal was now a common one—to oust the crusaders and retake Jerusalem and coastal Palestine. This was accomplished in 1187 under a young Kurdish officer named Saladin.

Mamluks

Saladin's victories over the crusaders made him a hero among his people. After his death in 1193, however, Saladin's army, comprised largely of Mamluk slaves, became disenchanted with their Ayyubid rulers. Mamluks were generally young slaves of Turkish or Mongol descent who had been purchased by the Ayyubids. By 1250, they had gained enough strength to be able to assume control not simply of the dynasty, but of the region. Within forty years, Mamluk forces succeeded in ejecting the last crusaders from Palestine.

The Mamluks ignored Palestine for much of their reign. As a result, two relatively quiet centuries passed under Mamluk rule. During this time, the Jewish population in Jerusalem grew. At the same time, as Europe was thriving and America was being discovered, the balance of world power began to slip further from the eastern Mediterranean.

The Ottomans

In 1516, Mamluk rule was brought to an abrupt end when the powerful armies of the Turkish Ottoman Empire entered the region, led by Selim I. The Ottomans were followers of Islam who created an empire that included Palestine and stretched from Algeria to Austria. Selim's successor, Süleyman the Magnificent, revived the Palestinian economy and rebuilt Jerusalem's city walls. Ruling the region for 400 years, the Ottomans were the last external power to have control of Palestine and the entire Levant—modern-day Lebanon, Israel, and parts of Syria and Turkey. "Levant" is a term that refers to the countries that lie on or near the eastern Mediterranean Sea.

Like the Mamluks before them, the Ottomans ruled Palestine as a province of Syria and had little interest in the area. European powers had not yet determined the value of this Middle Eastern land, either. All this would change in 1801 when Napoléon Bonaparte I of France landed his troops at Gaza, formerly a Philistine city on the Mediterranean coast of Palestine.

Napoléon intended to conquer Palestine as part of his eastward quest to incorporate all of Asia into his empire. A joint British and Ottoman force defeated Napoléon,

Even during the nineteenth century when Palestine was under Ottoman control, as seen in this 1826 map of Turkey, the Jewish Zionist movement was already beginning in Europe. When the empire was in decline after World War I (1914–1918), however, Britain—placed in control of Palestine by the League of Nations—was assigned to help the Jews establish their homeland. About 85,000 Jews lived in Palestine in 1914 and were then a minority group compared to the area's vast Arab population.

however. After this victory, Palestine sank back into obscurity, not rising to importance again until the end of the Ottoman Empire. At this time, Palestine became a pawn in the battles fought between the Turks and the British during World War I (1914–1918).

4 THE PRELUDE TO STATEHOOD

O nly small Jewish communities had remained in Palestine. The vast majority of the world's Jewish population lived in communities in Europe, elsewhere in the Middle East, Africa, and the Americas. Jewish nationalism among these Palestinian communities was growing, however.

Zionism and the First Aliyah

Beginning in the late nineteenth century, the oppression of Jews in Eastern Europe set off a mass emigration of Jewish refugees. These people eventually became known as the first *aliyah*. "Aliyah" literally means "ascent to the land." During the aliyah and unified in the belief that the Holy Land was theirs by destiny, the Zionist movement was established. The Zionists sought to make Palestine an independent Jewish nation.

MEDITERRANEAN
SEA

Tel Aviv

Jaffa

Gaza

EGYPT

This map shows Palestine and Transjordan (Jordan) under the British mandate and portions of Syria under the French mandate, and illustrates Jewish settlements prior to and during the British-controlled period (1881–1914). The terms of the British mandate obligated the British government to honor the Balfour Declaration of 1917, which pledged a homeland for the Jews in Palestine. In 1922, with the help of Winston Churchill, Transjordan was established as a separate emirate in which Jewish settlement was forbidden.

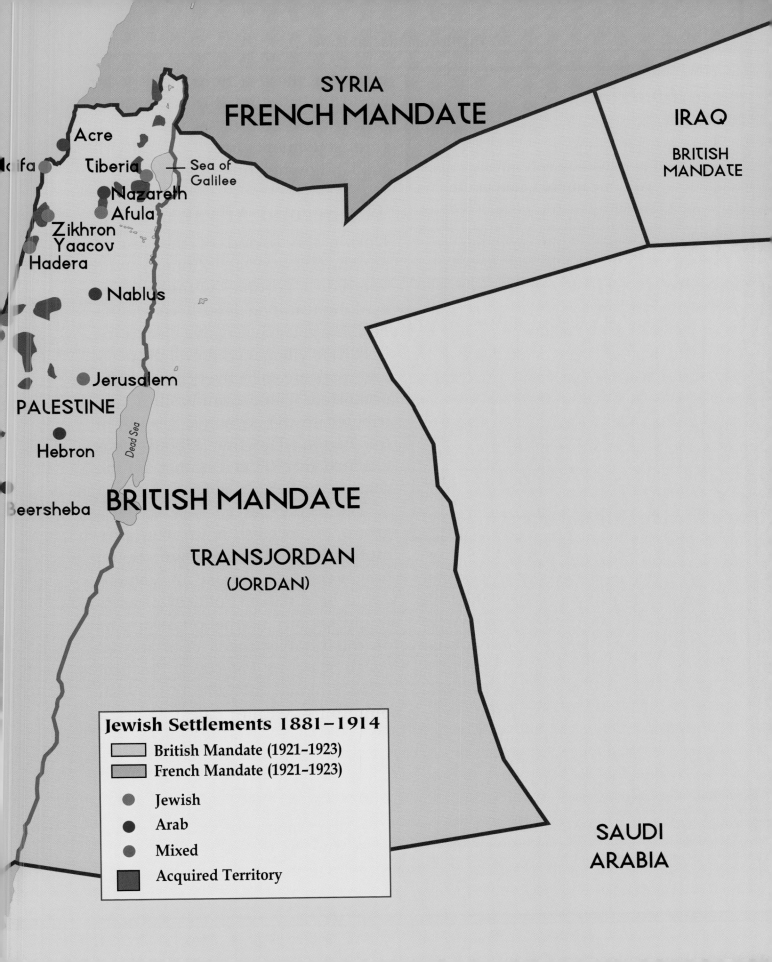

SYRIA
FRENCH MANDATE

IRAQ

BRITISH
MANDATE

Acre

Haifa

Tiberia

Sea of
Galilee

Nazareth

Afula

Zikhron
Yaacov

Hadera

Nablus

Dead Sea

Jerusalem

PALESTINE

Hebron

BRITISH MANDATE

Beersheba

TRANSJORDAN

(JORDAN)

SAUDI
ARABIA

Jewish Settlements 1881–1914

British Mandate (1921–1923)

French Mandate (1921–1923)

Jewish

Arab

Mixed

Acquired Territory

Kibbutzim

A *kibbutz* is a cooperative community where all property is collectively owned and work is collectively organized. All members contribute as workers and receive food, clothing, housing, and medical services. Dining rooms, kitchens, and stores are centralized, and schools and dormitories are communal. A kibbutz may be founded on agricultural, entrepreneurial, or industrial projects and elects leaders based on a majority vote.

The kibbutz is a derivation of the *moshav*, a similar cooperative settlement consisting of independent farms or community-owned land, where each family has its own house. Moshavim communities first appeared in Israel but gave way to the kibbutz when Britain and the Palestinians limited Jewish land ownership.

In 1897, the World Zionist Organization (WZO) convened in Switzerland. The aim of the WZO was to bring together international Jewry and publicize the cause of a national Jewish homeland. In 1901, the Jewish National Fund was founded to assist emigrating Jews to purchase land in Palestine. As a result of these actions, Jews who came to Palestine during the first aliyah were able to set up agricultural settlements based on individual land ownership, or *moshavim*.

The Second Aliyah

During the period of the second aliyah (1904–1914), Zionists who entered Palestine witnessed an evolution among Jewish communities. The moshavim gave rise to the *kibbutzim*, villages where all property and work are collectively owned and organized. These communities contributed to the economic growth of the region. The first kibbutz was founded in 1909 at Degania, on the coast of the Sea of Galilee.

The second aliyah was led by a group of socialist Jews who promoted Jewish nationalism. Soon, however, the Zionist movement would be divided. Political Zionists sought to gain international support for the establishment of a formal Jewish state in Palestine. Practical Zionists aimed to build the Jewish community within Palestine as a source of spiritual support for Diaspora Jewry.

This historic map, drawn by Joseph Perkins, shows boundaries in Palestine in 1826 when Ottoman Turks controlled the region. Among the districts included are Galilee, Batanea, Samaria, Peraea, and Judah.

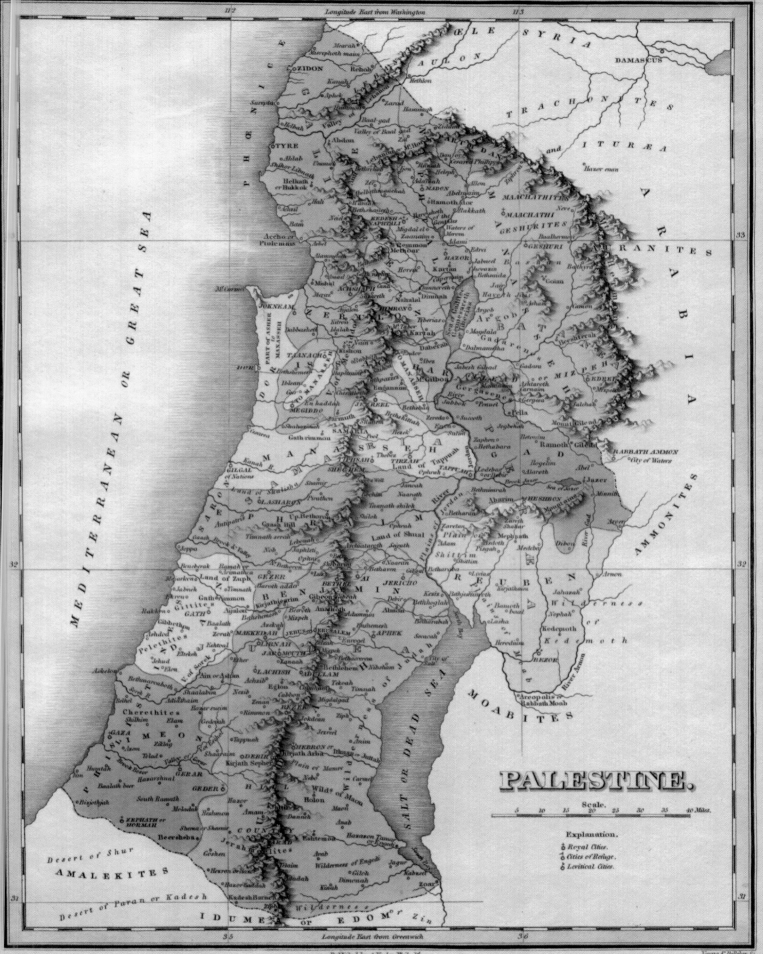

PALESTINE.

Scale.

Explanation.
Royal Cities.
Cities of Refuge.
Levitical Cities.

The Arab-Israeli Divide

In the early 1900s, 90 percent of Palestine's population was Arab Muslim. The Palestinians argued that since they were the majority and had lived in Palestine without disruption since the seventh century, they should be allowed to form an independent government there. By the onset of World War I, Palestine's population was about 700,000. Only about 85,000 of these inhabitants were Jewish.

As World War I began, Great Britain and her allies were looking for support from the Arabs and the Jews to topple the Ottoman Empire. The Ottoman ruler Muhammad V aligned his empire with the Germans. With the ongoing threat of war, the Allies were desperate for Middle Eastern assistance. In return for their support, both the Arabs and the Jews looked to Europe to support their territorial claims on Palestine. Both Jews and Arabs wanted complete control of the Palestinian territories.

By the end of the war, the Turks had been defeated and driven out of Palestine, but independence for Palestine did not come. The British government had made secret promises to both groups that were at best inconsistent and, at worst, deceitful.

Balfour and McMahon

In 1917, the leaders of Zionist movements in Britain and Palestine were made a promise. Known as the Balfour Declaration, written by British Foreign Secretary Arthur Balfour, it supported the creation of a national home for Jewish people in Palestine. This promise was made in return for Jewish support against the Ottoman Turks in World War I. Two years earlier, however, the British entered into an agreement with Middle Eastern Arabs that preyed on their desire for an independent Arab Palestinian state.

In a series of letters that came to be known as the McMahon correspondence, Britain secured Arab assistance in the ousting of Ottoman forces. In return, they were promised support in their efforts to obtain independence for Palestinian Arabs. In the end, neither agreement would be honored.

Then, unknown to both the Jews and the Arabs, Great Britain also made an agreement with France and Russia that divided the Middle East into permanent colonies to be ruled by Britain and France. Known as Sykes-Picot, this 1916 agreement superseded any other British promises regarding Arab independence or Jewish nationalism. After the war ended, the League of Nations (United Nations) divided the Ottoman Empire into

Haj Amin al-Husseini (1893–1974), exiled grand mufti of Jerusalem and leader of the Palestine Arabs from 1921, is pictured in this photograph taken in Karayel, Syria, as he prepares to make statements about the future of peace in the Holy Land. As president of the Supreme Muslim Council and former leader of Arab riots, he set upon following a pogrom to eliminate the presence of Jews in Palestine. The term "pogrom" means the willful devastation or destruction of a minority group, most often used when referring to the violent elimination of the Jewish people.

mandated territories. The territories of Mesopotamia (Iraq) and Palestine were mandated to the British, while Syria and Lebanon were mandated to the French.

While the Allies were dividing the spoils of the war, Jewish emigration into Palestine intensified. By the start of World War II (1939–1945), the population of Jews living in Palestine would jump from 70,000 to 450,000.

The Palestine Mandate

British control in Palestine began in 1920. Under the terms of the mandate, the British were to help the Jews build a national home, promoting Jewish self-government. Within two years, the League of Nations declared that the boundary of Palestine would be limited to the area west of the Jordan River. The area east of the Jordan River, the site of present-day Jordan, was made a separate British mandate.

The British government's fondness for the idea of a Jewish-controlled state in the Middle East was widespread. Not so much because they favored the Jews over the Arabs, but because they believed the Jewish state would be a British ally, or supporter. However, they underestimated the strength of Arab nationalism and the emerging economic importance of natural resources in the Middle East, such as oil.

This group of armed Jewish fighters prepares to face Arab rioters in Palestine during the 1938 Arab Revolt. Haj Amin al-Husseini led the Arab Revolt from 1936 to 1939, killing more than 400 Jews. Arabs under al-Husseini made specific demands of the British administration; Arabs wanted to end Jewish immigration to, and land purchases in, Palestine while increasing Arab representation in the country's government affairs. By 1939, the British government drafted the White Paper agreement that ended its 1918 commitment to Palestine.

Rising Jewish and Arab nationalism tested both British and French colonial rule. Despite growing tensions, Palestine saw nearly thirty years of development under David Ben-Gurion and his labor movement. Ben-Gurion dedicated his life to establishing a Jewish homeland in Palestine and became the nation of Israel's first prime minister in 1948. Today, Ben-Gurion is regarded as the father of modern Israel.

Arab Uprisings

As British control in Palestine progressed, Arabs became concerned about its growing Jewish population. The result of this concern was the formation of a national Palestinian Arab movement. Riots and demonstrations against both British policies and the Jews themselves followed.

Radical Zionists, including the Israeli terrorist group known as the Stern gang, and the Irgun, part of the Jewish Revolutionist Party under Menachem Begin, made the push to drive Palestinians from Palestine.

Arab leaders like the Grand Mufti of Jerusalem Haj Amin al-Husseini sought support for the termination of the British mandate and the elimination of all Zionist activity in Palestine. Growing Arab discontent culminated in the Arab Revolt of 1936 to 1939. At the same time, thousands of Jews were fleeing Germany to escape Adolf Hitler's Nazi movement.

In the years that followed, Israeli groups intimidated Palestinians in several massacres in which hundreds of Arabs were killed.

5 INDEPENDENCE AND CRISIS

With the onset of the Arab revolt, the British realized their World War I promises to the Jews and Arabs led to conflicting expectations. Although the British tried to appease both sides, the threat of war with Germany would soon take precedence. The rise of Adolf Hitler's Nazi movement would solidify the Arab-Jewish division in Palestine. It would also unify Jewish communities worldwide in their fight for an independent Jewish state in Palestine.

World War II

With Hitler's declaration to rid Europe of its Jews, hundreds of thousands sought refuge in Palestine. The British government was concerned that this mass migration would intensify an already delicate situation. Soon the British limited Jewish immigration. In a controversial document known as the White Paper, Britain imposed drastic restrictions on Jewish immigration and land ownership. The 1939 White Paper document also decreed that a joint Arab-Jewish government would be installed within ten years. These leaders would represent citizenry in proportion to the total population. Zionist leaders viewed this document as a reversal of the Balfour Declaration.

The Jewish men in this photograph lined up to be searched and sent on to Cyprus after they attempted to illegally enter Palestine in October 1947. Tensions between Arabs, European Jews, and the British were intensifying as more and more emigrants left Europe for Palestine. Finally, one month after this photograph was taken, United Nations officials recommended that Palestine be divided into separate Arab and Jewish states. This decision eventually terminated the British mandate over Palestine on May 15 1948, effectively creating the independent state of Israel.

The betrayal of the White Paper declarations did not dissuade Zionist leaders from entering World War II on the side of Britain and the Allied forces. The Arabs, disturbed by Britain's ambiguity on the issue of an independent Arab Palestine, entered the conflict in support of the German Nazis. It quickly became the most devastating war in human history.

During World War II, with the Nazi regime systematically mov-ing through Europe and imprisoning and murdering Jews, the United States became a center for Zionist activities. In 1942, a Zionist conference took place in New York. The meeting resulted in the establishment of the Biltmore Program, which rejected British restrictions in Palestine and called for the fulfillment of the Balfour Declaration. The British did not subscribe to the terms of the Biltmore, and restrictions on

Jewish immigration intensified. Nevertheless, between 1945 and 1948, about 85,000 Holocaust survivors were brought to Palestine by secret routes.

The Division of Palestine

In the aftermath of World War II, Britain looked to divest itself of Palestine completely. It passed administration of the region to the newly formed United Nations in 1947. A U.N. Special Committee on Palestine was then formed. After exhaustive debates, the committee agreed on a plan for partitioning Palestine between Arabs and Jews. The Partition Resolution was approved on November 29, 1947. It called for the creation of both an Arab state and a Jewish state within Palestine, west of the Jordan River. Jerusalem was to be governed by an international body.

Violence in Palestine increased while the United Nations debated partition. The result pleased no one. Palestinian Arabs rejected it outright. They claimed that too much land was being given to the Jews, considering their limited presence in the region. At this time the Jewish community comprised one-third of the population. Although the Jews accepted the decree, they also had no intention of honoring it.

Independence for Israel

On May 14, 1948, the day the British mandate over Palestine expired, Jewish authorities proclaimed an independent State of Israel. The declaration referenced the religious and spiritual connections of the Jewish people to the land, yet it did not denote its boundaries. David Ben-Gurion was named Israel's prime minister, and Chaim Weizman was

Israeli statesman David Ben-Gurion (1886–1973) was an active Zionist who led the political struggle for an independent Jewish state after World War II. Ben-Gurion eventually became the first prime minister of Israel, serving from 1949 to 1953 and again in 1955 to 1963. Although he resigned twice after that, once in 1961 and again in 1963, he remained politically active throughout his senior years, forming political parties and writing about his experiences.

SYRIA

Acre

Haifa

Sea of
Galilee

Nazareth

MEDITERRANEAN
SEA

Nablus

Jordan River

Tel Aviv

Amman

Jericho

Jerusalem

Dead Sea

Gaza

Hebron

Beersheba

Negev Desert

JORDAN

SINAI
PENINSULA

Israel in 1949

Israeli Territory

Eliat Aqaba

named its president. The United States, the United Soviet Socialist Republics (USSR), and many other nations recognized Israel.

Just one day later, however, the nations of the Arab League attacked Israel. The Arab League was then made up of seven Arab countries (Iraq, Saudi Arabia, the Lebanese Republic, Yemen [San'a], Transjordan [Jordan], Egypt, and Syria) and was created for the purpose of coordinating international Arab policy. It was also formed to curb aspirations for a Jewish national state in Palestine. The combined Arab armies fought the Jewish-led Israel Defense Forces (IDF) in what became known as the first Arab-Israeli War. The fighting ended in 1949 when Israel and each of its bordering states signed a cease-fire agreement. The truce also outlined the borders of the new State of Israel.

In addition to establishing boundaries, the first Arab-Israeli conflict also extended Israeli-controlled lands past borders determined by the United Nations. Portions of the territory designated for Palestinian Arab control, Gaza and the West Bank, ended up in the hands of the Egyptians and Jordanians, respectively. Jerusalem was divided between Israel and Jordan, with the new city under Israeli control and the old walled city remaining in Jordanian hands.

The new balance of power caused several hundred thousand Arabs to flee Israel for Gaza, the West Bank, and neighboring Arab countries. Although permanent peace negotiations were supposed to follow the cease-fire, they did not. The Arabs refused to recognize, much less negotiate with, Israel.

A Period of Peace

The majority of the world, however, did recognize the independence of the new nation. In May 1949, Israel joined the United Nations, and its next seven years were largely peaceful.

In 1950, Israel affirmed the right of every Jew to live in Israel, and promoted unrestricted immigration. In the first four months alone some 50,000 immigrants—mostly Holocaust survivors—arrived in Israel. By the end of 1951, that number neared 700,000 and included Jews from Europe and Africa. Israel's Jewish population had nearly doubled. Mass immigration compounded Israel's

This map depicts Israel after the War of Independence (1947–1949) against Lebanon and Syria in the north, Iraq and Transjordan (Jordan) in the east, and Egypt in the south. More than 6,000 Israelis were killed in the conflict. In 1948, the United Nations agreed to create an independent Jewish state. After the war, the new State of Israel held its own, and by 1949, it had even increased its territories by approximately 50 percent.

The Arab-Israeli Conflict

The dispute between Arabs and Jews over Palestine is referred to as the Arab-Israeli conflict. This conflict has led to a number of wars among Arab nations, Palestinian refugees, and the State of Israel. The Arab-Israeli War of 1948–1949 included the armies of Egypt, Transjordan, Syria, Lebanon, and Iraq as well as Palestinian guerrillas. In 1967, Egypt, Syria, and Jordan massed their armies on Israel's borders for the Six-Day War. Also known as the October or Ramadan War, the Arab-Israeli War of 1973 had Israel fighting the armies of Syria and Egypt.

Since that time several peace accords have addressed the conflict, beginning with the 1979 Camp David Accords, but a real resolution seems unlikely.

Former Israeli Prime Minister Menachem Begin makes remarks on the South Lawn of the White House during one of his frequent visits to Washington, DC. Former President Jimmy Carter is seen behind him.

economic strain, and the nation searched for international support from the United States and other countries.

Israeli politics remained stable through the 1950s; however, the lack of peace settlements between Israel and its neighbors caused continual tension. Skirmishes between Israelis and Arabs in Gaza and the West Bank were ongoing. Israel held Jordan responsible for the attacks and engaged in retaliation. Soon Syria and Egypt would also be involved in these conflicts.

The Suez Crisis

In 1952 a young Egyptian army colonel, Gamal Abdel Nasser, seized power in Egypt. Nasser promoted a highly emotional brand of pan-Arabism. Pan-Arabism is a movement for greater cooperation among Arab or Islamic nations. The goal of pan-Arabism is to unify the Arabic-speaking masses into one state powerful enough to take control of Palestine.

One of Nasser's first actions was to nationalize the Suez Canal and refuse

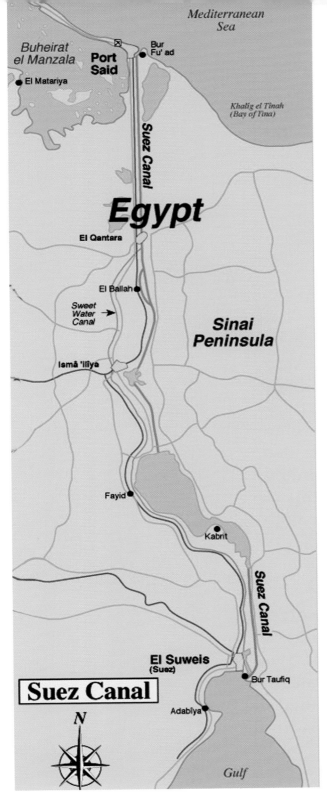

This contemporary map illustrates the Suez Canal, a 120-mile-long (193-kilometer-long) canal—the longest in the world—responsible for the second-largest exchange of foreign trade. The Suez has been the site of three wars: the 1956 Suez Crisis, the 1967 Six-Day War, and the 1973 Yom Kippur War.

to allow access to Israel. The Suez Canal connects the Mediterranean Sea with the Red Sea. Early in his reign beginning in 1956, Nasser began to acquire weapons from the Communist government of Czechoslovakia and to intensify Arab guerrilla campaigns against Israel.

Israel was being crippled by the combination of increasing border fighting and the restriction on trade resulting from the closing of the canal. To fight back, Israel participated in secret negotiations with Britain and France and engaged in a plan to regain access to the Suez.

On October 24, 1956, Israel invaded the Gaza Strip and the Sinai Peninsula. As had been agreed, Britain and France demanded that both Israeli and Egyptian forces withdraw from the Suez. When Nasser refused, British and French forces bombed Egypt. The United States and the USSR demanded an immediate cease-fire. Shortly thereafter, the United Nations forced the entirety of British, French, and Israeli forces out of the Suez. Finally, the Egyptian government reopened the Suez and Israel regained access to the Strait of Tiran and the Red Sea.

6 WAR AND PEACE

decade of peace followed once the Suez crisis ended, although no Arab-Israeli negotiation talks resumed and border incidents continued. Despite these battles, Israel's economy and foreign relations developed rapidly. Israel also increased its military might. The United States agreed to supply Israel with arms in 1962, and West Germany provided both economic and military aid.

The Six-Day War and the PLO

By the mid-1960s, however, unresolved issues from continual tensions between Israel and the Arabs had intensified again. In 1964, the Arab League created the Palestine Liberation Organization (PLO) headed by Yasser Arafat. The goal of the PLO was the liberation of Palestine.

EGYPT

This map shows territories gained by Israel in the Six-Day War in 1967 and the Arab-Israeli War of 1973. The Israeli occupation of these territories increased the rate of Palestinian refugees who emigrated into surrounding Arab nations, especially into Jordan.

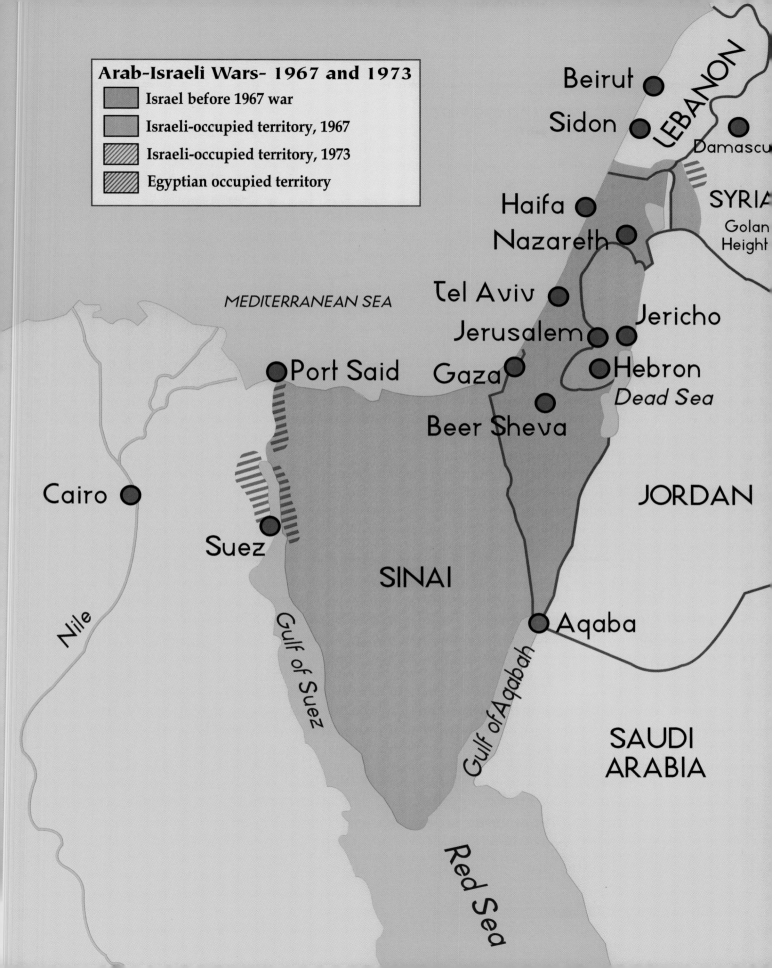

Arab-Israeli Wars– 1967 and 1973

- Israel before 1967 war
- Israeli-occupied territory, 1967
- Israeli-occupied territory, 1973
- Egyptian occupied territory

LEBANON

Beirut

Sidon

Damascu

SYRIA

Golan Height

Haifa

Nazareth

Tel Aviv

Jerusalem

Jericho

Hebron

Gaza

Dead Sea

Beer Sheva

MEDITERRANEAN SEA

Port Said

Cairo

Suez

SINAI

JORDAN

Aqaba

Gulf of Suez

Gulf of Aqabah

Nile

SAUDI ARABIA

Red Sea

The Palestine Liberation Organization

The creation of the State of Israel in 1948 and the wars between Israel and Arab nations displaced many Palestinians. The Palestine Liberation Organization (PLO) is the political body that represents the Arab people of Palestine and was founded in 1964 as a channel for Palestinian demands for a state.

The PLO grew in regional and international prominence after Arab armies proved unable to defeat Israel in the Six-Day War of 1967 and Israel occupied the Gaza Strip and West Bank. Arab governments designated the organization in 1974 as the "sole, legitimate representative of the Palestinian people." Later that year, the United Nations also recognized the PLO as the representative of the Palestinian Arabs.

Yasser Arafat (1929–) founded Al Fatah, an underground terrorist organization, in 1956, and in 1968, became the leader of the PLO. Having become less of an aggressor by the 1980s, Arafat recognized Israel as an independent state in 1988. After the Oslo Peace Accords in 1994, he went on to win the Nobel Peace Prize along with Yitzhak Rabin and Shimon Peres of Israel. In 1996, Arafat was elected president of the Palestinian Council governing the West Bank and Gaza Strip.

In 1965, the Palestinians began armed attacks against Israel. Israel responded with raids against Syria and Jordan. In 1967, after creating alliances with Syria, Jordan, and Iraq, Nasser moved his troops into the Sinai Peninsula and again closed the Strait of Tiran to Israeli shipping.

In retaliation, Israeli forces launched a military strike against Egypt on June 5, 1967. Both sides accepted a U.N. cease-fire just six days later. In the end, Israel had taken control of the Golan Heights from Syria, the Sinai Peninsula and the Gaza Strip from Egypt, and the West Bank and East Jerusalem from Jordan. Israel's new boundaries were short-lived, however, when the U.N. called for Israeli withdrawal from the territories occupied at the conclusion of the Six-Day War.

The aftermath of the 1967 Israeli victory saw the emergence of concealed Palestinian resistance in the form of terrorism. The PLO became

A member of the International Olympic Committee (*bottom right*) speaks with a masked Palestine Liberation Organization (PLO) terrorist. Palestinian terrorists invaded the Olympic Village in Munich, Germany, kidnapping and killing two athletes while holding nine other athletes hostage. The following morning all nine Israelis were killed in a shootout between terrorists and West German police officers.

the sole representative of the Palestinian people and pledged to liberate Palestine by any means necessary. To demonstrate their commitment to Arab independence, the PLO carried out bomb attacks and hijackings throughout the 1970s. The most notorious was the massacre at the 1972 Munich Olympics in which eleven Israeli athletes were killed.

Despite condemnation of PLO-sponsored terrorism, the world did recognize the Palestinian cause. In 1974, the Palestinian National Council (PNC), the body responsible for electing PLO leaders, decided to revisit its policies for the attainment of a liberated Palestine. It decided to settle for a Palestinian state in the West Bank and Gaza Strip.

The Yom Kippur War

Israeli and Egyptian forces engaged in intense border fighting along the Suez Canal between 1969 and 1970. When Egyptian President Gamal Nasser died in 1970, the newly elected president, Anwar Sadat, attempted to regain the Sinai Peninsula from Israel through diplomatic means. However, negotiations failed. On October 6, 1973, Yom Kippur, the holiest of Jewish holidays, Egypt and Syria attacked Israeli positions in Sinai and the Golan Heights. Perhaps because of its swift victory in the 1967 Six-Day War, Israel suffered tremendous losses.

Within days, Egyptian forces had crossed the Suez Canal and swept through the Golan Heights. Despite this success, Israeli forces were able to defeat the Arab army. The war ended a month later when, on October 25, 1973, a United States–sponsored cease-fire went into effect.

Attempts at Peace

The shock of near defeat in the Yom Kippur War motivated Israel to negotiate a peaceful compromise with its Arab neighbors. Unfortunately, it also motivated an investigation into Israel's lack of leadership and military strength. The results of the investigation were highly critical of the military and

The injured Israeli soldier seen in this photograph, taken by photographer David Rubinger in the Golan Heights, was caught in an ambush of gunfire in the first days of fighting against Syrian soldiers in the Yom Kippur War in 1973. Replacement Israeli soldiers were being sent in to relieve the first soldiers who had taken the brunt of the initial attacks.

Golda Meir (1898–1978) is seen in this photograph speaking at a National Press Club luncheon in 1974. Meir was prime minister of Israel from 1969 to 1974, immediately following the death of Levi Eshkol. Meir resigned from the post in 1974 following criticism she received for Israel's lack of preparedness after the Egyptian-Syrian invasion during the 1973 Yom Kippur War.

prompted the resignation of Israeli Prime Minister Golda Meir.

In 1977 the new Israeli prime minister, Menachem Begin, called for the leaders of Jordan, Syria, and Egypt to end the dispute. President Sadat of Egypt accepted. That same year, Sadat made an unprecedented visit to Israel. In return for this gesture, Begin went to Egypt. Two years later, in a deal brokered by the United States, President Jimmy Carter led the historic Egypt-Israel Camp David Peace Treaty of 1979.

The treaty was a framework for peace across the Middle East, and it addressed the future of the West Bank and the Gaza Strip, as well as Israel's relationship with Jordan. Despite the promise of peace between Egypt and Israel, the two sides were unable to make substantial progress. In fact, most Arabs reacted negatively to the treaty.

The members of the Arab League saw Egypt's formal recognition of Israel as disloyal. In 1981, Sadat was assassinated by one of his own men. His successor, Hosni Mubarak, had been against the peace agreement. Although he maintained the terms of the treaty, the relationship between the two countries was best characterized as a "cold" peace.

Hostilities continued between Israel and other Arab nations. Israel's border with Lebanon, however, had been relatively quiet during the previous Arab-Israeli wars. Beginning in the 1980s, tensions between Lebanese Muslims and Christians were heightened by the arrival of both the PLO and Syrian forces into Lebanon.

7 MODERN CONFLICTS

In 1982, at the recommendation of Ariel Sharon, Israeli minister of defense, Israel launched a major military action into southern Lebanon. The objectives of the raid (called Operation Peace for Galilee) were to ensure security for Israel and to destroy the PLO bases in Lebanon. Within months, the Syrian PLO forces had been defeated and the PLO withdrew from Lebanon.

Afterward, hundreds of Palestinian men, women, and children were massacred in Lebanese Palestinian refugee camps at Sabra-Shatila near Beirut. Christian Phalangists, a right-wing Lebanese religious group, carried out the killings, but the IDF failed to intervene. Israeli outrage over the massacre resulted in Begin's resignation in 1983. Despite an overwhelming disapproval of Israel's actions in Lebanon, Israel maintained a military presence there until 1985

This map shows territories gained by Israel in the Six-Day War in 1967 and the Yom Kippur War of 1973. Israeli forces continued to occupy the Gaza Strip and the Sinai Peninsula, and added the Golan Heights of Syria, the West Bank, and East Jerusalem. This incursion against Egypt and Syria led to a response from Arab troops out of Jordan. By 1973, Arab-led troops attacked Israeli positions in Sinai and the Golan Heights during the Jewish holiday of Yom Kippur. Israeli troops continued to hold sway, however, and controlled the Suez Canal while driving Syrian armies back toward Damascus. Israeli Minister of Defense Ariel Sharon (1928–) *(inset)* became Israel's prime minister in 2001.

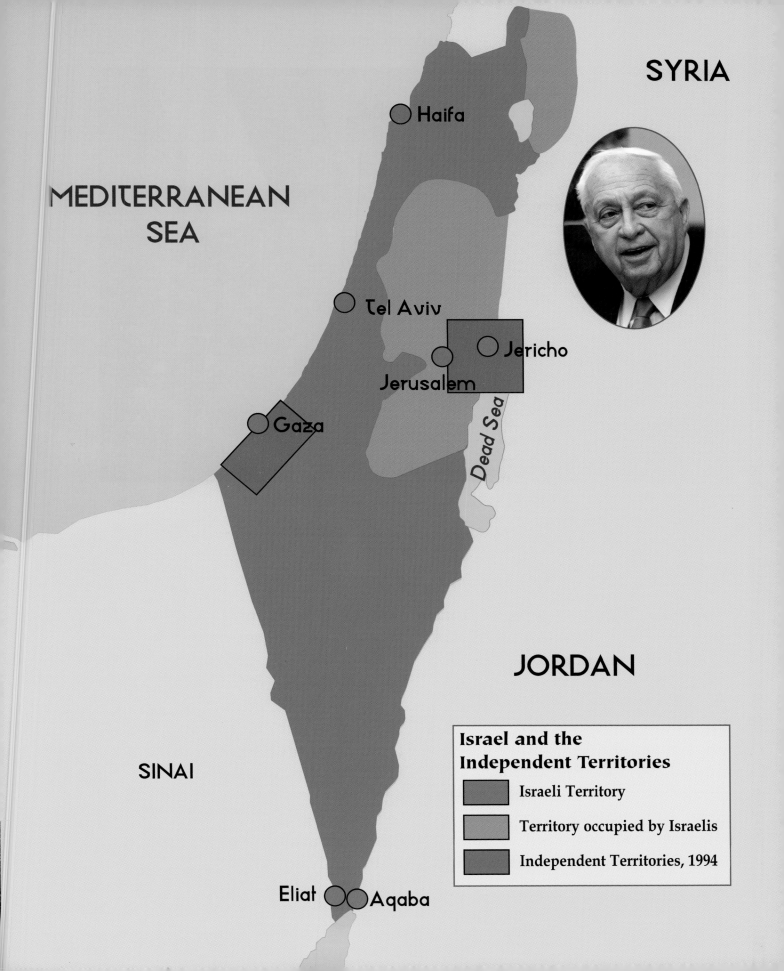

SYRIA

⬤ Haifa

MEDITERRANEAN
SEA

⬤ Tel Aviv

⬤ Jericho

⬤ Jerusalem

Dead Sea

⬤ Gaza

JORDAN

SINAI

**Israel and the
Independent Territories**

Israeli Territory

Territory occupied by Israelis

Independent Territories, 1994

Eliat ⬤⬤ Aqaba

A woman from Brussels, Belgium places candles forming the words "Sabra" and "Shatila" in this contemporary photograph. Her efforts mark the twentieth anniversary of the Sabra and Shatila Massacre in which hundreds of Palestinians were killed in refugee camps in Lebanon. This memorial service took place at the Palace of Justine in Brussels on September 14, 2002.

through a six-mile-wide buffer zone. Israeli withdrawal from Lebanon would not occur until 2000.

A Unified Government

Yitzhak Shamir replaced Begin as prime minister in 1983. When the elections of 1984 failed to produce a clear winner, the two main parties—the Israeli Labor Party and the more conservative Likud—agreed to form a unified government for fifty months. The two candidates, Shimon Peres and Yitzhak Shamir, shared duties. Peres first served as prime minister.

The unified government succeeded. Israeli forces in Lebanon were reduced, and inflation was brought under control (largely due to a $1.5 billion loan from the United States and a new free trade agreement). Several attempts at securing peace across the Middle East were also attempted.

In 1987, in response to twenty years of Israeli rule and Jewish

Yitzhak Rabin (1922–1995), prime minister of Israel from 1974 to 1977 and 1992 to 1995, won the 1994 Nobel Peace Prize along with Shimon Peres and Yasser Arafat for the negotiation agreements known as the Oslo Accords. The accords recognized Israel's right to exist and the right of the Palestinians to be represented by the PLO. Rabin served Israel publicly—both militarily and as a politician—for most of his life. An Israeli student who sought to halt the peace process in the Middle East assassinated him in November 1995.

settlement in the occupied territories, Palestinian resistance efforts became more aggressive. Under the PLO, rioting and unrest developed into the first *intifada*, or uprising. As the movement expanded, Israel's increasingly harsh responses to Palestinian acts came under international criticism. Efforts by Israeli Defense Minister Yitzhak Rabin and U.S. Secretary of State George Schultz to initiate peace negotiations failed.

After seven months of intense fighting, responsibilities related to the Israeli-occupied, Jordanian-controlled West Bank were ceded to the PLO. In response, Israel immediately restricted the activities of Palestinian institutions. In response, the PLO unilaterally proclaimed an independent state of Palestine, with Jerusalem as its capital, and recognized the right of Israel to exist by accepting U.N. Security Council Resolution 242. The PLO's Arafat was named president of the State of Palestine.

When the 1988 elections took place, it was again too close to call.

Another unified government would be installed, however this time just one leader would hold power. Shamir was to remain prime minister, and Peres became the minister of finance. Rabin remained minister of defense.

The 1990s

In 1990, however, Israel's unified government began to collapse. The Knesset, the parliamentary legislature of Israel, terminated the Shamir government in the country's first-ever no-confidence vote. Shamir became the leader of a right-wing coalition committed to the preservation of a Jewish Israel, not an integrated one.

One month after the declaration of an independent Palestine, Israel announced elections in the West Bank and Gaza. The Israelis recognized the need for greater Palestinian independence in the occupied region. The Israelis' proposal, however, raised little confidence. Many wondered how the elections would be held and whether Israel's full withdrawal from Palestine would be discussed. Before long, however, Iraq invaded Kuwait and the resulting Persian Gulf War again divided the Arab world.

The Persian Gulf War

In August 1990, Iraqi forces occupied Kuwait. This conflict between Iraq and an international coalition of forces led by the United States raged throughout 1991.

As the war intensified, Israel found itself in an unusual position. Although it was a war between Arab countries, Iraq's Saddam Hussein needed to divide the coalition, so he attacked Israel. His goal was to engage Israel in the war and thus show his Arab rivals as supporters of Israel. The United States–led alliance against Hussein encouraged Israel *not* to retaliate. When it did not, Hussein's plan failed.

On February 24, 1991, the attack of coalition forces began. Operation Desert Storm lasted precisely one hundred hours. In the end, Iraqi forces were defeated and Kuwait was liberated.

Quest for Peace

After Operation Desert Storm, the 1990s produced several milestones to peace. Iraq's defeat by the United States–led alliance made peace in the Gulf region a priority. Soon, the world's focus turned to the

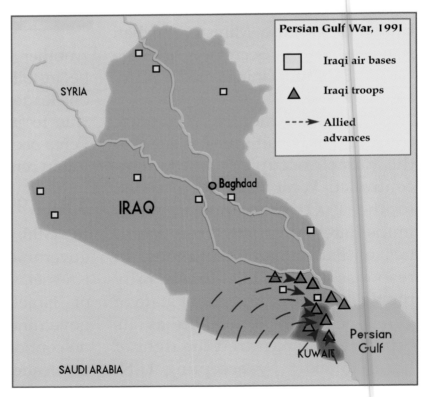

In 1991, Saddam Hussein attempted to drag Israel into the Persian Gulf War by attacking the nation and forcing some Arab countries such as Syria, Egypt, the United Arab Emirates, and Saudia Arabia to feel as though they were a part of a coalition that supported the Jewish nation.

Arab-Israeli conflict and international peace initiatives.

United States Secretary of State James A. Baker brought together Israeli Prime Minister Shamir and representatives of Syria, Jordan, Lebanon, Egypt, and a delegation of Palestinians at the Madrid Peace Conference. In the aftermath of these talks, much of Asia initiated diplomatic relations with Israel for the first time. The United Nations also reversed a resolution that equated Zionism with racism.

Unfortunately, progress slowed as Shamir and his right-wing government expanded Israeli settlements in the occupied territories. A confrontation with the United States was narrowly averted by the election of Yitzhak Rabin in July 1992. A year later, during a U.S. ceremony in Washington, D.C., the Israelis and Palestinians signed a declaration known as the Oslo Accords. Mediated by former President Bill Clinton, Arafat and Rabin sealed the deal with a handshake.

The agreement outlined the PLO's affirmation of Israel's right to exist in peace and Israel's recognition of the PLO as the representative

James A. Baker III (1930–), secretary of state under President George H. W. Bush from 1989 to 1992, made diplomatic strides in the Middle East following the Gulf War (1990–1991). After many visits to the region, his efforts resulted in the invitation to representatives from Israel, Syria, Lebanon, Jordan, Egypt, as well as the Palestinians, to the Madrid Peace Conference in 1991. Besides the obvious issue of decreasing tensions in the region, the talks promoted a dialogue regarding environmental and economic issues.

of the Palestinian people. The PLO also renounced the use of terrorism and other forms of violence, and it agreed to resolve conflicts with Israel through peaceful negotiations.

The accords also delineated a proposal for limited Palestinian self-rule in Gaza and the West Bank town of Jericho. It also stated that within five years an agreement would be reached regarding all remaining territories in dispute, including Jerusalem. The PLO established the Palestinian National Authority (PNA) to administer these regions.

8 ISRAEL TODAY

I n October 1994, Israel and Jordan also signed a peace treaty that focused on security, boundaries, and water resources. Both parties agreed not to join, aid, or cooperate with any party intending to attack the other side and to work together to combat terrorism. They also agreed to solve the problem of Palestinian refugees. Finally, Israel recognized Jordan's role as guardian of Muslim holy places in Jerusalem. This angered Palestinians because it seemed to undermine their agreement with Israel to later negotiate the status of Jerusalem.

Although initial progress was substantial, the process would derail in 1995 when an Israeli student assassinated Prime Minister Rabin. Shimon Peres, who had been serving as foreign minister under Rabin, then became prime minister. For several months, the peace process continued.

This current map of Israel shows its present boundaries, along with its occupied territories in the Golan Heights (also claimed by Syria) and in the West Bank and Gaza Strip. Despite years of peace initiatives between Israel and surrounding Arab nations, violence continues to erupt between rival Israeli and Palestinian forces. In 2002, Israelis reoccupied some areas of the West Bank that they had surrendered in the 1990s. These sections, agreed Israel, would eventually be subject to Palestinian self-rule.

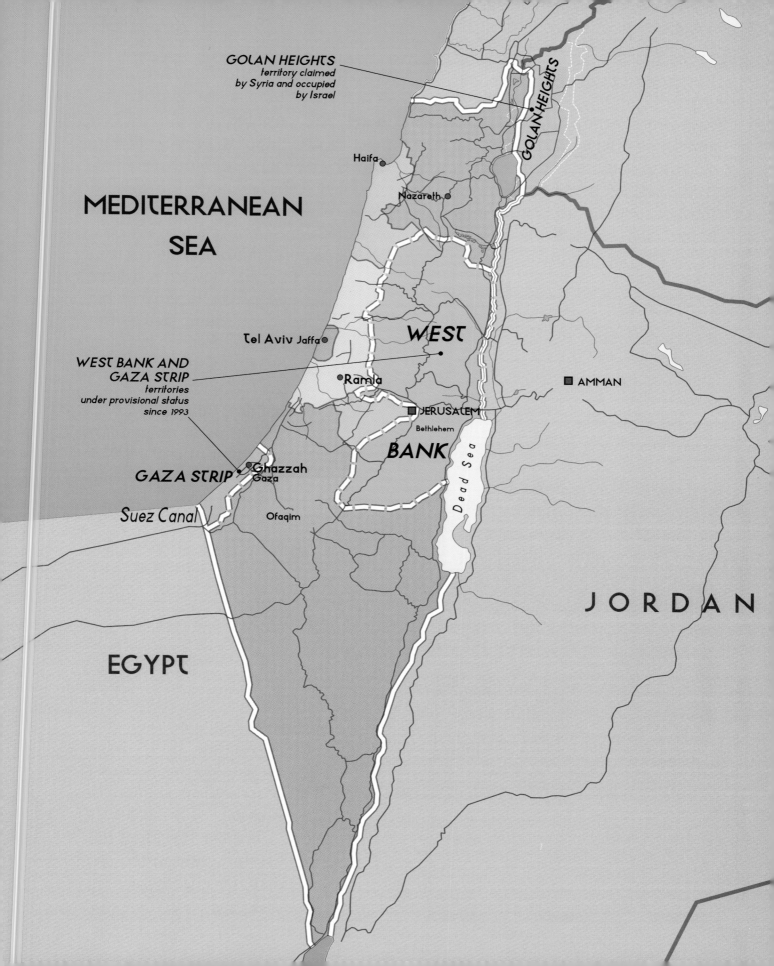

MEDITERRANEAN
SEA

GOLAN HEIGHTS
*territory claimed
by Syria and occupied
by Israel*

GOLAN HEIGHTS

Haifa

Nazareth

WEST

Tel Aviv Jaffa

**WEST BANK AND
GAZA STRIP**
*territories
under provisional status
since 1993*

Ramla

□ AMMAN

□ JERUSALEM

Bethlehem

GAZA STRIP Ghazzah
Gaza

BANK

Dead Sea

Suez Canal

Ofaqim

J O R D A N

EGYPT

Progress Pauses

Palestinian groups initiated terrorist attacks against Israel in 1996. As tensions intensified, Peres made fewer compromises in the name of peace. In May 1996, Likud leader Benjamin Netanyahu soundly defeated Peres in the country's general election. He formed a coalition government determined to assure security for Israel and insisted that the PNA meet its obligation to prevent terrorism. The peace process again stalled.

The first Palestinian elections took place in 1996. Yasser Arafat was voted in as both president and leader of the PNA. Support for Arafat was not universal, however. Many people believed that his negotiations with the Israelis were not on behalf of Palestine but for securing his own political future.

The main opposition to Arafat and the PNA comes from the Islamic group Hamas. Hamas was founded in 1988 as a militant wing of the Muslim Brotherhood, an organization that advocates an increased role of Islam in government, and rejects Western influences. They flatly protest the peace process and, since self-rule began in 1994, have staged several terrorist actions with the intent to stop it.

Former President Bill Clinton attempted to rekindle discussions in

This map is a U. S. Central Intelligence Agency (CIA) map from 2001, which shows Israel's boundaries, as well as Israeli-occupied territories in the Golan Heights, West Bank, and Gaza Strip. These territories remain subject to negotiation.

1998 by bringing together Israel's Netanyahu and Palestine's Arafat. The men agreed to meet but were unable to reach an agreement. When Israel's 1999 elections came around, Labor Party candidate Ehud Barak defeated Netanyahu.

With Barak installed as prime minister, so came the promise of "bold steps" in forging a comprehensive peace plan for the Middle East. He focused on negotiations with the Palestinians and expressed eagerness to reach an agreement with Syria. He also promised to withdraw the remaining Israeli troops from southern Lebanon by 2000. Although these steps brought optimism to the long-stalled process, ultimately they would accomplish little to foster peace.

Barak did transfer some West Bank territory to the PNA, but by November 1999 negotiations stalled again, with both sides caught up in percentages of land to be transferred. In December 1999, Israel and Syria agreed to meet as well, based on Barak's hint that he would return the Golan Heights to Syria in exchange for peace. Talks held in January 2000, however, were inconclusive and a follow-up summit between Syrian President Bashar Assad and former U.S.

Former President Bill Clinton stands between Yitzhak Rabin and Yasser Arafat during the signing of the Israeli-Palestinian Declaration of Principles, part of the Oslo Accords, on the South Lawn of the White House on September 13, 1993.

President Clinton also failed to end the stalemate.

The Second Intifada

Frustrated by increased terrorism in the Middle East by 2000, the United States convened a summit in which Clinton, Barak, and Arafat focused on peace agreements.

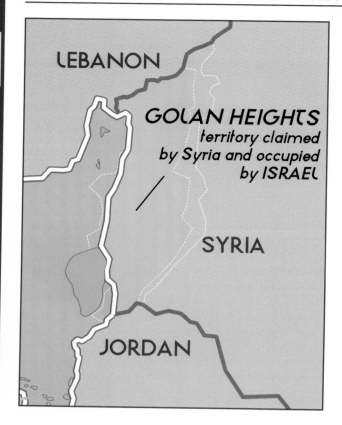

LEBANON

GOLAN HEIGHTS
territory claimed by Syria and occupied by ISRAEL

SYRIA

JORDAN

The Golan Heights, an area stretching about 444 square miles (1,150 square kilometers) is a strategic territory that has been occupied by Israeli forces and settlements since 1967. Still claimed by Syria and not recognized as Israeli territory by international law, the land represents about 1 percent of Syria's overall nation. The Golan Heights is a thriving area that currently provides Israel with more than 30 percent of its water supply.

An Ancient Divide

Sharon's government wanted to stop the violence and restore security in Israel. He firmly believed that the violence must stop before negotiations for peace could continue. Palestinian suicide bombings and other terrorist activities continued in Israel, however, and the peace process seemed hopeless. The September 11, 2001, terrorist attacks on New York and Washington, DC, reinforced the desperate need for peace in the Middle East.

In 2002, Israeli forces swept into the West Bank and reoccupied key urban centers. During the three-week operation, Israeli forces arrested hundreds of alleged terrorists and destroyed weapons. At the time of this writing, devastating terrorist attacks against men, women, and children were occurring with unfortunate regularity in Israel. People of every religion and ethnicity have been and are still being killed.

The failure of the summit led to the outbreak of the second intifada, also known as the Al-Aqsa intifada after the holy Al-Aqsa Mosque in Jerusalem. Unlike the first intifada, the Al-Aqsa intifada was characterized by vicious Palestinian attacks on Israeli civilians and subsequent Israeli military responses. In reaction to the second intifada, Israeli public opinion shifted to the right. Barak resigned in December 2000, and in February 2001 center-right politician Ariel Sharon, a vocal critic of returning the West Bank and Gaza Strip to Palestinian control, was elected prime minister.

An Israeli border policeman *(left)* and a Palestinian scream at each other in this dramatic photograph taken in the Old City of Jerusalem on October 13, 2000. Israelis prevented thousands of Palestinians' entry to the Al-Aqsa Mosque for Friday prayers over concerns of continued unrest and clashes between Israelis and Palestinians following traditional Muslim services. Tensions between both groups intensified during fighting in the West Bank and Gaza Strip.

A Possibility for Peace

Considering the cycle of violence responsible for the shape of Israel today, true peace in the Middle East may never be possible. Although each new government brings hope that the violence and bloodshed will end, Israel is a nation so rooted in religion that a lasting peace would need to address questions that may be difficult to answer.

For now, Israel continues fighting for freedom. Although in its independence it has achieved a national Jewish homeland, Israel has not attained a declaration of independence of, or peaceful cooperation with, the Arabs of Israel and neighboring Arab nations.

TIMELINE

10000–6000 BC Human settlements are established in the Jordan Valley.

3200–2150 BC Writing develops in Mesopotamia; major cities of Jerusalem are built.

1550–1250 BC Time of Hebrew enslavement in Egypt.

1290 BC Hebrews receive the Torah at Mount Sinai.

1250 BC Moses leads the Israelite Exodus from Egypt.

1000 BC David conquers Jerusalem, bringing with him the Ark of the Covenant.

928 BC Division of the Israelite state into the kingdom of Israel and Judah.

586 BC Judah defeated by Babylonians under Nebuchadnezzar.

333 BC Alexander the Great conquers Jerusalem.

AD 30 Jesus Christ is crucified.

70 Roman Empire seizes Jerusalem; Jewish residents are sent into exile.

325 Constantine converts to Christianity; Palestine is recognized as the Holy Land.

644 Palestine becomes Islamic territory.

1099 Crusaders establish a kingdom in Jerusalem.

1187 Saladin defeats the crusaders.

1516 Palestine becomes part of the Ottoman Empire.

1880s Jewish immigrants begin to arrive in Palestine from eastern Europe.

1914–1918 World War I; Israel as part of Palestine sides with Germany.

1920–1948 Period of the British Mandate.

1947 U.N. recommends partitioning Palestine.

1948 The State of Israel declares independence.

1949 David Ben-Gurion becomes Israel's prime minister.

1956 Israel sides with Great Britain and France to overthrow Nasser in Egypt; invades Sinai and Gaza.

1967 The Six-Day War against Syria, Egypt and Iraq begins.

1973 The Yom Kippur War in October.

1978 The Camp David Accords are signed.

1981 Egyptian President Anwar Sadat is killed by Islamic militants.

1982 Israel invades Lebanon.

1987 The first intifada.

1990–1991 The Persian Gulf War.

1995 Rabin and Arafat sign interim peace agreement; Rabin assassinated.

1996 Benjamin Netanyahu becomes Israeli prime minister.

1997 Hebron is handed over to Palestinian control.

1999 Ehud Barak becomes prime minister.

2000 Second intifada.

2001 Ariel Sharon becomes prime minister.

2002 Israeli forces reoccupy the West Bank.

2003 Ariel Sharon reelected.

GLOSSARY

aliyah A Hebrew word meaning to return.

bedouin Wandering Arabs who live in the deserts of the Middle East.

Canaan The ancient name for what is now the State of Israel.

covenant Agreement.

diaspora Derived from the Greek word meaning "to be dispersed"; refers to Jews forced into exile.

Exodus The departure of the Israelites from Egypt under the leadership of Moses.

Gaza Strip A region in the Mediterranean, bordered by Egypt and Israel.

guerrillas Members of a band of fighters who harass the enemy by sudden raids or ambushes.

idolatry The worship of idols or false gods.

Jerusalem A historic city lying at the intersection of Israel and the West Bank; claimed by Israel as its capital.

Levant The countries about the eastern Mediterranean Sea from Greece to Egypt, especially Syria, Lebanon, and Israel.

Mamluks Slaves converted to Islam who advanced themselves to high military posts in Egypt.

masada A fortress; specifically, an ancient ruined fortress in Israel.

Muslim A follower of the Islamic faith.

Palestine A historic region situated on the eastern coast of the Mediterranean Sea in southwestern Asia. Palestine is now largely divided between Israel and the Israeli-occupied territories.

Palestine Liberation Organization (PLO) A political body working to create a state for Palestinian Arabs in some or all of Palestine, a historic region now comprising Israel and the Israeli-occupied West Bank and Gaza Strip.

Promised Land Refers to Israel as the land God promised to the Jews in return for their promise to worship Him.

Ramadan In the Islamic calendar, the ninth month of the year, made up of thirty days.

regent A person who rules a country when the rightful ruler cannot, either because he or she is too young, out of the country, or ill.

terrorism The use or threat of violence to create fear or alarm.

schism A split or division.

Torah The first five books of the Bible: Genesis, Exodus, Leviticus, Numbers, and Deuteronomy; a body of Jewish teachings.

United Nations An international organization of countries created in 1945 to promote world peace, cooperation, and human rights.

West Bank Territory in southwestern Asia, bounded on the north, west, and south by Israel and on the east by Jordan.

Zionism A worldwide movement, originating in the nineteenth century, that sought to establish and develop a Jewish nation in Palestine.

FOR MORE INFORMATION

Center for Middle East Peace
633 Pennsylvania Avenue NW,
5th Floor
Washington, DC 20004
(202) 624-0850
Web site: http://www.centerpeace.org

Web Sites

Due to the changing nature of Internet links, the Rosen Publishing Group, Inc., has developed an online list of Web sites related to the subject of this book. This site is updated regularly. Please use this link to access the list:

http://www.rosenlinks.com/liha/isra

FOR FURTHER READING

Cahill, Mary Jane. *Israel* (Major World Nations Series). Philadelphia: Chelsea House Publishers, 1999.

Fisher, Frederick. *Israel*. Milwaukee: Gareth Stevens, 2000.

Green, Jen. *Israel*. Austin, TX: Raintree Steck-Vaughn, 2002.

Landau, Elaine. *Israel* (Enchantment of the World Series). New York: Children's Press, 1999.

Stefoff, Rebecca. *West Bank/Gaza Strip*. Philadelphia: Chelsea House Publishers, 1999.

Wagner, Heather Lehr. *People at Odds – Israel and the Arab World*. Philadelphia: Chelsea House Publishers, 2002.

BIBLIOGRAPHY

Fodor's Israel. 5th ed. New York: Fodors LLC., 2001.

Frank, Harry Thomas, ed. *Atlas of the Bible Lands*. Union, NJ: Hammond World Atlas, 1990.

Hellander, Paul, Andrew Humphreys, and Neil Tilbury. *Israel and the Palestinian Territories*. Australia: Lonely Planet, 1999.

Lee, Risha Kim, ed. *Let's Go: Israel and the Palestinian Territories*. New York: St. Martin's Press, 2002.

Stannard, Dorothy, and Brian Bell, eds. *Insight Guide Israel*. London: Insight Guides, 1999.

Reich, Bernard. "Israel," World Book Online Americas Edition. Retrieved October 2, 2002 (http://www.worldbookonline.com/ar?/na/ar/co/ar282960.html).

"Israel." CIA-World Fact Book. Retrieved October 2, 2002 (http://www.cia.gov/cia/publications/factbook/geos/is.html).

"Israel (country)." Microsoft® Encarta® Online Encyclopedia 2002. Retrieved October 2, 2002. (http://msn.encarta.com).

"Israel, country, Asia." The Columbia Encyclopedia, 6th ed., 2001. Retrieved September 30, 2002 (http://www.bartleby.com/65/is/Israel.html).

"Israel." Infoplease.com. Retrieved September 30, 2002 (http://www.infoplease.com/ce6/world/A0825647.html).

"Israel: a country study." Retrieved September 30, 2002 (http://lcweb2.loc.gov/frd/cs/iltoc.html).